SCIENCE IN THE
KITCHEN

Rebecca Heddle

Edited by Helen Edom

Designed by Susie McCaffrey

Illustrated by Kate Davies

Consultant: Julie Deegan

Contents

Experimenting in the kitchen

Lots of exciting scientific things happen in your kitchen every day. This book will help you to find out about these things. The first experiments are about cleaning up.

Cleaning birds

Sea-birds can get covered in spilled oil, which water cannot wash off by itself. People use a cleaner like dishwashing liquid to remove the oil.

Helping to mix

Try this experiment to find out how dishwashing liquid helps to make things clean.

1. Smear a little butter on a plate. Hold the plate under the cold faucet. Does the water make the plate clean?

Does the water mix with the butter?

2. Add a little dishwashing liquid to the butter and mix it in with your fingers.

3. Hold the plate under the faucet again. What happens this time?

Does the water still roll off the butter?

Dishwashing liquid helps water to mix with things better than it can on its own. This is how it helps to make things clean.

Making bubbles

Mix four large spoonfuls of dishwashing liquid into a small glass of water.

Twist a piece of thin wire to make a loop with a handle. Dip the loop right into the mixture. What do you see when you take it out?

Look carefully at the loop.

Blow steadily through the loop, and watch what happens.

Dishwashing liquid can spread out very thin. This is why it can stretch across the loop. It can even stretch around the air you blow out, to make a bubble.

Washing bubbles

Dishwashing liquid stretches around tiny pockets of air trapped in running water. This is how it makes bubbles on the water.

Spreading out

Try this to see how far dishwashing liquid can spread out.

Sprinkle talcum powder on a bowl of water. Add a drop of dishwashing liquid. Watch what happens.

The dishwashing liquid pushes the talcum powder away as it spreads out over the surface of the water.

3

Soaked through

What things do you use to mop up spills? They need to be good at soaking up water.

Dish-cloth **Tissue** **Tracing paper**

Soaking up

Collect different things, to see which soaks up water best. Here are some things you could try.

Try to find pieces about the same size.

Cotton

Pour a teaspoon of water onto a saucer. To test each thing, put it on the water. Count to five, then take it away. Does it soak up all the water?

Coffee filter paper

Plastic

Use a new spoonful of water for each test.

Some things leave water behind. Dry the saucer before you test each thing.

Feeling the difference

Feel a dry piece of each thing you tested. The things that soak up water feel rougher than the things that don't, because they are full of tiny holes. The holes let the water in.

Sponges

Bathtub sponges soak up water very well. You can see the holes that let the water in.

4

Marble test

Try this strength test on three or four things that soak up water. Secure each one over an empty plastic jar with a rubber band. Put a marble on top.

Drop a spoonful of water on each marble, and watch what happens.

Do the marbles move?

Which marble sinks down the least?

Some things get weak when they are wet and let the marble drop. Things that mop up well need to stay strong.

Soaking colors

See what happens when water soaks through colours from markers.

You need: strips of coffee filter paper, markers (dark colors are best), saucer.

Put a big color dot near one end of each paper strip.

Pour some water into the saucer. Put the colored end of each strip in the water. Watch what happens.

Is the color the same all the way up?

Most colors are made up of other colors. They separate out as water soaks through them.

5

Disappearing water

Have you ever wondered what happens to the water in wet things when they dry?

Drying out

Soak two dishcloths in water and wring them out so they are just damp.

Feel the cloths the next day. Which one is driest?

Spread one cloth on a plate. Put the other in a plastic bag and tape it shut. Leave them in a warm place. Which cloth do you think will dry first?

Wet things dry out because tiny water drops escape from them into the air. This is called evaporation.

The cloth in the bag stays wet, because the water cannot reach the air.

Getting water back

Look at the bathroom mirror when you have had a bath.

What can you see? Touch the glass. Is it wet?

Water evaporates from your bathtub. When the tiny drops in the air hit something cool, like the mirror, they join up to make drops that you can see.

Salty water test

Stir two teaspoons of salt into a small bowl of warm water. Taste a tiny bit of the water to find out how salty it is.*

Cover the bowl with clear plastic and leave it in a warm place.

Look at it after an hour. What do you see on the inside of the plastic?

This water has evaporated from the bowl.

Taste the water on the plastic.* Is it salty?

When water evaporates, anything mixed in it is left behind.

Never taste things unless an adult says they are safe to eat.

Rainbow sugar

You can use evaporation to make colored sugar crystals to eat.

You need:
2 spoons of sugar,
10 spoons of water,
food color,
foil dishes or
saucers covered
with foil.

Stir the sugar into the water until it disappears.

Pour two spoonfuls onto each foil dish.

Add a different food color to each dish. Leave the dishes in a warm place for three days.

The water evaporates and leaves behind colored sugar crystals. You can break them up and mix them to make rainbow sugar.

7

Wet and dry

Most food has water in it. Some food is dried to take the water out.

Pop the lid

Find a small plastic container with a lid. Fill it with dried peas, and pour in cold water up to the top.

Stand the container on a saucer, and put on the lid.

Look at the container the next day. What has happened? Take out the peas. How much water is left?

Each pea has gotten much bigger.

The peas get big enough to push the lid off the container because they take in water. Dry food can soak up lots of water.*

Knock down the tower

Make a tower of four sugar cubes on a plate. Add a little food coloring to some water. Pour it onto the plate and watch what happens.

Watch the bottom of the tower.

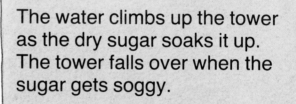

The water climbs up the tower as the dry sugar soaks it up. The tower falls over when the sugar gets soggy.

The color helps you see how high the water climbs.

8

* The peas must be soaked overnight and cooked to make them good to eat.

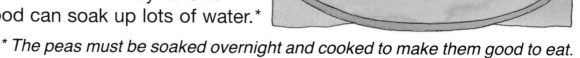

Drying things out

Sprinkle sugar on a slice of cucumber. Leave it for ten minutes. Has anything changed?

Can you see water on the cucumber?

Sugar soaks up water so well that it can draw water out of cucumber.

Drying to keep

Try this experiment to find out why food is dried.

Cut a slice of bread in half. Leave one piece in a warm, sunny place until it feels dry. Sprinkle water on the other piece.

Put each piece in a clear plastic bag. Tape the bags loosely shut. Label them "wet" and "dry".

Cellophane tape

Leave the bags in a warm place. Look at them after four days to see if any mold has grown. Which piece is the most moldy?*

Keep the bags closed all the time.

Mold

Mold grows best on wet food. Food is dried so that mold does not grow on it so quickly. This means it can keep for a long time.

Throw the bags away when you have finished the experiment.

Adventure food

Explorers take dried food with them, because it keeps for a long time and it is light to carry.

9

Juice

Every sort of fruit has juice in it. Juice is mostly made up of water.*

Looking at juice

Look at an orange segment. Does it feel wet? Can you see the juice inside it?

Orange segment

Hold the segment over a plate and squeeze it very hard. Can you feel the juice now?

Is the juice the same color as the orange? Does it taste the same?

Is the segment in your hand as big as before?

Juice takes up most of the space in fruit. It has most of the color and flavor in it.

Water in everything

Every living thing, including you, has water in it. Your body is about two-thirds water.

Getting juice out

See how easy it is to get juice out of different sorts of fruit. Here are some you could try.

Kiwi fruit

Raspberry

Blackberry

Apple

Lemon segment

Pear

It may help if you squash the fruit with a spoon.

Juice is held in tiny bags called cells. You have to break the cells to get it out. The cells in some sorts of fruit are harder to break than others.

An orange's cells are big enough to see, and easy to break.

* *These experiments are messy, so wear old clothes to do them.*

Colorful juice

You can do this experiment with brightly colored juice, like raspberry or blackberry juice. You also need an old white cotton handkerchief.

Make a simple pattern on the handkerchief with colorful juice. Leave it to dry.

Next day, wash the handkerchief under the tap. Can you still see any color?

The color in juice can stain material. It is very hard to wash off.

Invisible ink

Draw a picture on white paper with lemon juice. The picture is hard to see when it is dry.

Keep dipping your finger in the juice.

Ask an adult to iron your invisible picture with a hot iron. The picture appears almost instantly, because the heat from the iron turns the lemon juice brown.

Picture after ironing

Dyes

People can use juice from fruit, flowers, or bark to make cloth interesting colors. Juice colors are called natural dyes.

Taste tests

The way food tastes helps you decide whether you like eating it.*

Tongue test

You taste things with your tongue. It tells you whether things are sweet, like sugar, or bitter, like coffee.

Make sure your hands are clean for this test.

Dip a finger in powdered sugar. Dab it on the back of your tongue, then one side, then tip. Where does it taste sweet?

Back of tongue

Sides

Tip of tongue

Rinse your mouth with water. Now test cold black coffee in the same three places. Where can you taste the bitterness?

Different parts of your tongue notice sweet tastes and bitter ones.

Smelling taste

Why doesn't food taste as good when you have a cold? Try this to find out.

You need a blindfold and two drinks with straws in them. You could try strawberry and banana milkshakes.

Ask someone to blindfold you. Hold your nose and taste one drink, then the other. Can you tell which is which?

Your tongue can only tell you that both the drinks taste sweet. It cannot tell them apart.

*Never taste things unless an adult says they are safe to eat.

Try the test again, but don't hold your nose. Can you taste the difference now?

Your nose notices different flavors that your tongue cannot taste.

You cannot tell flavors apart when you have a cold because your nose is blocked.

Treading on taste

Flies taste food with their feet. They walk all over food to find out if it is good to eat.

Funny colors

Colors help you to guess how food will taste before you eat it. See what happens if you change the color of food.

Use food coloring to make food funny colors. You could give people green scrambled eggs, purple mashed potato and blue milk.

Watch their faces as they taste the food. Do they want to eat it?

If food is a funny color, you think it will taste horrible. This helps to keep you safe, because food sometimes changes color when it goes bad.

13

Sour things

Acids are chemicals that can be dangerous. But lemons and other foods have safe, weak acids in them. They tend to taste sour.*

Tasting sourness

Taste different sorts of food and drink to see which might be acid. Here are some things you could try. Can you guess which ones will taste sour?

Vinegar

Milk

Soft drink

Water

Orange

Salt

Yogurt

Sugar

Grapefruit

Try making a chart to show which things taste sour.

taste sour

vinegar
soft drink

14

Red cabbage test

You can make red cabbage water to help you test for acid food.

You need: half a red cabbage, hot water, saucepan, strainer, clean jug, jars or glasses.

Tear the red cabbage leaves into little pieces. Put them in the saucepan.

Ask an adult to pour boiling water into the saucepan. Let it cool for half an hour.

Pour the cabbage water through a strainer into a jug.

You don't need the cabbage bits.

Look at the cabbage water to see what color it is. Pour some into each jar.

* Never taste things unless an adult says they are safe to eat.

Add some lemon juice to one jar. Does anything change?

Red cabbage water changes color from purple to pink when you add acid to it. Things that are not acid leave the cabbage water purple or turn it green.

Try adding the other things that taste sour to jars of red cabbage water. Do they all turn it pink?

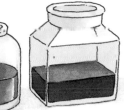

Now try adding the things which do not taste sour. Are any of them acid?

Some acid things, like soft drinks, don't taste sour because there is lots of sugar in them.

* Don't drink the cola. Throw it away.

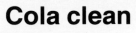

Cola clean

Drop a dirty copper coin into a glass of cola.

Take out the coin the next day. Has it changed?

Is the coin still dirty?

The acid in cola is strong enough to eat away the dirt on the coin.*

Pickled food

Keeping food in vinegar is called pickling. The acid in vinegar stops food from going bad, so you can keep it for a long time.

15

Fizz

Have you noticed tiny bubbles in soft drinks? Try these experiments to find out more about these bubbles.

Going up

Pour some clear soft drink into a big jar. Can you see the bubbles? They are full of gas.

Drop in some raisins and watch what happens.

Bubbles stick to the raisins. The gas in them is so light that they can carry the raisins to the top of the drink.

The bubbles burst at the top. The light gas escapes, so the raisins sink. More bubbles stick to them at the bottom, and they go up again.

Making a fizz

This experiment uses baking soda. It is used in baking, and you can buy it at the supermarket.

Put a spoonful of vinegar in a glass. Sprinkle in a spoonful of baking soda. Watch what happens.

When you mix an acid*, like vinegar, with baking soda, gas fizzes out.

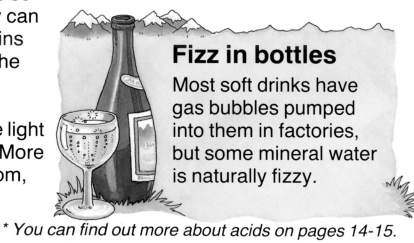

Fizz in bottles

Most soft drinks have gas bubbles pumped into them in factories, but some mineral water is naturally fizzy.

16

You can find out more about acids on pages 14-15.

Fizz in your mouth

You can make a sweet treat that fizzes with citric acid, which you can buy at a pharmacy or wine-making shop.

You need:
2 spoons of citric acid crystals,
1 spoon of baking soda,
8 spoons of powdered sugar, bowl.

The acid and baking soda can only fizz together when they get wet. The wetness in your mouth makes the mixture fizz.

Mix up the ingredients in a bowl. It doesn't fizz until you put a little dab in your mouth. Then you can feel the gas escaping.

Test this by dropping water on a spoonful of the mixture.

Heat bubbles

Carefully pour some very hot faucet water into a clear heat-proof bowl. Add a spoonful of baking soda.

You will need to look very closely to see the tiny bubbles.

Baking soda can fizz without acid when it gets very hot.

Cake bubbles

The holes in a piece of cake are bubbles made by baking soda in the cake mixture.

The baking soda makes the bubbles when the mixture gets hot in the oven. This makes the cake rise.

17

Dough

When you mix flour with oil and water, you make it into something completely different, called dough. Here you can find out more about dough.

Modeling dough

You need:
10 heaped tablespoons all-purpose flour, 1 teaspoon salt, 4 teaspoons oil, 8 tablespoons warm water, bowl.

Mix the flour and salt in a bowl. Pour in the oil. Add the water bit by bit, mixing it in with your other hand.

Stop adding water if the dough gets sticky.

Adding heat

You can make models from modeling dough. If you want to keep them, ask an adult to help you bake them.*

The heat in the oven turns the dough hard.

Stretch and squash the dough until it all holds together.

Does it feel like flour now? How many differences can you find? You could write them on a chart.

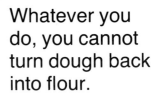

flour	dough
dry powdery	wet squashy

Whatever you do, you cannot turn dough back into flour.

Dough for bread

If you add yeast to flour, water and oil, you can make dough for bread.

Make sure your hands are clean.

You need:
flour, oil,
warm water and salt
as for modeling dough,
3 teaspoons of
dried yeast,
1 teaspoon sugar,
a glass, bowl,
baking tray,
plastic bag.

Mix the flour and salt. Pour in the oil and the yeast mixture. Slowly add the rest of the water. Mix and squash the dough.

Shape the dough into six rolls. Put them on a baking tray.

Mix the yeast and sugar in the glass. Stir in half the warm water.

Cover the tray with a plastic bag. Put it in a warm place. Look at the rolls after 20 minutes. Are they still the same size?

Leave it for 15 minutes. Watch what happens.

Gas bubbles

The rolls get bigger because the yeast makes bubbles in the dough.

Yeast is a living thing. When it has sugar, water and warmth, it grows and makes bubbles of gas.

Take off the plastic bag, and ask an adult to cook the rolls.*

When the rolls have cooled, break one open and look inside.

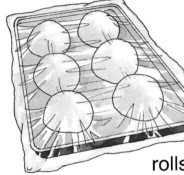

The bubbles of gas have left holes in the rolls.

* See page 23 for cooking times and temperatures.

Freezing and melting

Water changes into ice when it gets very cold. Can you guess what happens to other things?

Frozen food

Food can be kept frozen for months. When it is warmed up again, it is still good to eat.

Making things cold

Put a spoonful or a small lump of different things in the sections of an ice cube tray. Put it in the freezer.*

You could try: tomato ketchup, fruit juice, syrup, oil, milk, cheese, butter, chocolate.

Take the things out after two hours. Tip them onto a tray. Has anything changed?

Feel things to find out how hard they are.

Most things get hard, like ice, when they get cold enough. This is called freezing.

Ice to eat

A popsicle is like a frozen drink on a stick. The warmth in your mouth makes the popsicle melt.

Some things, like oil, need to be very cold indeed before they freeze. Even the freezer may not be cold enough to make them go hard.

Is anything still runny?

* You could use the ice-making compartment of a refrigerator.

20

Warming up

Frozen things soften when they warm up. Some things get runny when you take them out of the freezer. This is called melting. Try this to see if ice always melts at the same speed.

You need:
2 mugs,
2 ice cubes,
cotton,
plastic wrap

Wrap one mug in cotton. Put an ice cube in each mug and cover them both with plastic wrap.

Leave the mugs in a warm room. Which ice cube do you think will melt first?

Look at the mugs every ten minutes to see if you are right.

Oven mitts

Oven gloves help to keep heat out. People wear them to protect their hands from hot things.

The ice cube in the unwrapped mug melts first because warmth from the room gets in quickly. The other ice cube stays frozen longer because warmth cannot get through cotton so quickly.

21

Notes for parents and teachers

These notes are intended to help answer questions that arise from the activities on earlier pages.

Experimenting in the kitchen (pages 2-3)

Like most things, water and dishwashing liquid (detergent) are made up of molecules. Detergent molecules are long, and only one end of them attracts water molecules. The other end attracts other things, like butter and dirt. This is how detergent makes a link between water and things which do not dissolve in water.

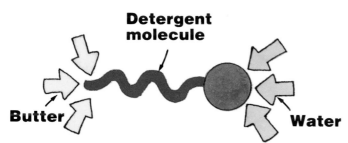

Detergent molecule

Butter

Water

Detergent spreads out over the surface of water because the detergent molecules line up, each with one end away from the water.

Detergent molecules

Water

Soaked through (pages 4-5)

Water molecules attract each other very strongly, so when a little water moves into a gap in a fabric, its molecules pull in more water. This helps water to soak into things.

Disappearing water (pages 6-7)

When water evaporates, its molecules move into the air. They spread apart, forming invisible water vapor. When water vapor touches a cool surface, the molecules join together again to make small water drops that you can see. This is called condensation.

Wet and dry (pages 8-9)

Mold and bacteria are living things that need water to survive. This is why drying food tends to prevent them from growing, and so preserve the food.

Bacteria that need air to live are less dangerous than the sort that don't need air. The bags of bread must only be sealed loosely so air can get inside, to encourage the safer sort of bacteria to grow. You should still take care, and keep the bags closed even when you are throwing them away.

Taste tests (pages 12-13)

Different areas of your tongue have taste buds that detect different basic tastes, and send messages to your brain about them. There are four basic tastes – sweet, bitter, sour (like lemon juice), and salty. You can test sour and salty tastes in the same way as sweetness and bitterness. This tongue map shows the areas where each taste can be detected.

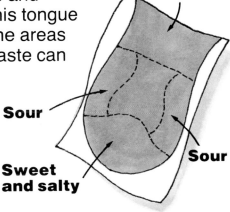

Bitter

Sour

Sour

Sweet and salty

Sour things (pages 14-15)

Red cabbage water is an indicator. This means that it changes color when it is mixed with acids or other chemicals called alkalis. Alkalis turn it greeny-blue. Baking soda is a safe alkali that you can test, but most alkalis in the kitchen are cleaning substances and may not be safe to handle.

Red cabbage water mixed with baking soda

If you mix acid and alkali in the right proportions, they neutralize each other, and have no effect on cabbage water.

Neutral things leave red cabbage water purple.

Dough (pages 18-19)

Cooking instructions - bake modeling dough models at 180°C, 350°F, Gas mark 4 for 30 minutes. They will only keep for a long time if they are really dried out. Bake rolls at 230°C, 450°F, Gas mark 7 for 15 minutes.

Yeast is a fungus. In dried form, it is dormant, but providing it with warmth, water and food (sugar) reactivates it. It produces carbon dioxide bubbles which become holes in the bread. The yeast is killed by the intense heat in the oven so the bread stops rising.

Freezing and melting (pages 20-21)

Cotton doesn't let heat through quickly because it contains trapped air, which does not conduct heat well. Other spongy materials also make good insulators.

Trapped air between the cotton fibers

23

Index

First published in 1992 by Usborne Publishing Ltd., Usborne House, 83-85 Saffron Hill, London, EC1N 8RT, England. www.usborne.com Copyright© 2006, 1992 Usborne Publishing Ltd.

The name Usborne and the devices 🔱 🎈 are trade marks of Usborne Publishing Ltd.
Printed in China. AE.